MW00596454

HARD
WORK

or

Harmony?

*A Go-To Guide for Women to
Nurture Healthy Relationships With
Family, Friends, and Co-Workers*

Kiaundra Jackson, LMFT

Hard Work or Harmony?

A Go-To Guide for Women to Nurture Healthy Relationships with Family, Friends, and Co-Workers

Copyright © 2020 Kiaundra Jackson

All Rights Reserved. No portion of this book may be reproduced, stored in a retrieval system or transmitted in any form or by any means- electronic, mechanical, photocopy, recording, scanning or other- except for brief quotations in critical reviews or articles, without the prior written permission of the publisher.

ISBN: 978-0-9992081-0-6

For more information, please visit:
www.KiaundraJackson.com

TABLE OF
CONTENTS

INTRODUCTION

C an you imagine waking up, opening your eyes to the world, and saying thank you to God for allowing you to see another day? Before getting out of bed, you feel an external glow and internal happiness. Girl, you are feeling good! You start your morning routine by brushing your teeth, washing your face, putting on your clothes, and eating a healthy breakfast. As you take one final look in the mirror before leaving home, you feel confident. It is not because you are cocky or "big-headed," it's because you realized something...

Today is unlike any other day.

You realize a number of things. You slept well. You fell asleep easily, didn't wake up in the middle of the night, didn't have any unpleasant dreams, and got up without hitting the alarm's snooze button. You were motivated to start your day; there were no disrespectful text messages on your phone, no voice messages from anyone with a nasty attitude, and no emails from anyone with whom you had unresolved issues. You log onto social media, there are no negative comments or DM's (direct messages) or people saying anything untrue about you. You feel good (and you look good too lol). Before you start to feel overly confident or think that you are perfect, you realize the sum of all these events is based on one thing--your relationships are healthy!

Not only that, but it is also because the different areas of your life are correctly aligned. When you look at the various aspects of your life: mentally, spiritually, emotionally, financially, and relationally, you realize they're blossoming and blooming. They have shown so much change and progress that you hardly believe this is your life. There isn't any stress or dysfunction. Your relationships with your family members are good. You talk to them as needed. You set boundaries and expectations for them. They check in on you, and you check in on them. You get together when time and circumstances allow. You video chat, call, text, email, and stay connected via social media. There is no turmoil; there is no drama; there is no discord. You feel at peace.

What about your romantic relationships? I know some of you may be boo'd up. Whether you're in a relationship or not... it's healthy, it's growing, it's not struggling at all. In fact, it is thriving! Situations that may cause friction or bring you to a place of disagreement are fully rectified because you utilize effective communication skills.

What about your work relationships? You walk into work feeling amazing. There isn't anyone next to your cubicle or in the organization that you have discord with. Your workday flows effortlessly. You walk out of work with your hair blowing in the wind because you are content. You are content because these situations in your life weren't always okay, but now they are. This is what healthy, harmonious relationships look like in the different aspects of your life.

Your money is flowing. You consistently have enough money to cover your bills and any additional living expenses because you have made good choices with your spending and savings.

Your thoughts, feelings, and emotions are in check, and you feel on top of the world. And you look great because when you feel good on the inside, it is reflected on the outside.

But wait!

Can you imagine if this wasn't a one-day feeling but something you exuded, amplified, and experienced daily? It may seem unbelievable, but it is possible.

This is possible for you.

It is not about perfection; it is about progression. It is possible when you realize the circumstances in your life don't always have to be the way they have always been. You may be looking at your relationships now, thinking, "Yep! I am good in this area. My relationships are pretty good." If so, I want to encourage you to look a little deeper. There are always areas of life that can be improved. There may even be a relationship that has always been a little rocky, but you have pushed it to the side, thinking it will fix itself.

Or you may know your relationships need tons of work, and you will NOT deny it one bit.

Before we go any further…

Take a deep breath!

Take a deep breath because you need it. I mean you REALLY need it. You have been working so hard to "hold it all together" that you are exhausted. Girl, you have been trying to juggle multiple roles as a mother, spouse, employee, friend, sister, daughter, and so on for a while now. Let's be honest! We both know it is not working too well for you. You are not just exhausted, but you are overwhelmed to the point you lack the energy to push forward. But, you do it anyway because you are trying to be a superwoman.

You cannot hold space for all these different roles and different people--without giving YOURSELF the same grace you give to others. Before you give up, muster a little more strength to deal with the only thing you can control--YOU!

I will deal with the guys another time, but this book is just for the ladies. In this book, I will present some simple, easy to implement strategies to help you heal yourself to have healthy relationships with family, friends, and co-workers. I am confident that after reading and embracing this book's content, you're going to be on a much better path. All you have to do is lean into it. Even though you may not agree with everything I initially say, do not write it off as foolery. Be willing to implement what I share. All you have to do is just try it.

I know this may feel like hard work, but it does not have to feel that way. Embrace the desire for the life that you want to live and commit yourself to do the work to achieve it.

Let's dive into how to nurture healthy relationships with family, friends, and co-workers by first making sure there is harmony.

Chapter 1
CONNECTED BY BLOOD, CHOICE, OR MARRIAGE

Relationships are unique. They are so unique that when I use the word "relationships," your mind probably went to the romantic ones. If you did, shame on you! (just kidding, there is no judgment here). But, this is why I chose to shed light on some of the most crucial relationships in our lives. Throughout this book, you will hear me call them connections or interpersonal relationships. No matter which words I use, keep in mind that I am referring to family, friends, and co-workers. Interpersonal relationships come in different forms, manifest in different ways, and connect us with different types of people. From my perspective, being connected with others is one of the greatest gifts on earth. That gift is even greater when the people you are connected with are also healthy or striving to be so.

Let me give you a set of my own definitions and extra tips for the different types of relationships to ensure we are on the same page.

Friendships: A relationship where there are no formalities, and individuals enjoy each other's presence.

Extra Tip: Friendships can vary in length of time. You can have friends you have known forever and friends you just met who are equally special to you.

Romantic Relationships: A relationship where individuals are attached to each other and share a special bond. This bond is usually characterized by passion, intimacy, trust, respect, and love.

Extra Tip: Romantic relationships can occur in multiple stages: dating, exclusivity, engaged, newlyweds, and marriage. The stage you are in does not take away from the amount of romance you produce.

Family Relationships: Individuals related by blood or marriage are said to form a family. Some individuals can be classified as "family" without being blood-related.

Extra Tip: An example is a long-time friend of your parents you have known for years and consider an aunt or uncle.

Professional (Work) Relationships: Individuals working together for the same company or organization are typically referred to as co-workers or colleagues. Professional relationships can also include those who do not work with you or are in the same field/professional capacity.

- Employee to Employee
- Employer to Employee

Extra Tip: Coworkers and colleagues are not mandated to like one another (lol)

Harmony: A consistent, orderly, pleasing arrangement of parts; there is an agreement, things are on one-accord; harmonious relations; congruity.

Relationships are not always what we think they are, nor do they have all of the elements we believe they should have which makes them complex and prevents any two from being the same. You may be asking yourself, "Well, what makes them so different, and why aren't they the same?" You are the common denominator in all of your relationships. How we show up in relationships is a direct reflection of the work we have done on ourselves to create personal harmony that extends into interpersonal relationships.

How we handle relationships as adults stem from our childhood.

Let that sink in for a moment. It does not matter if it was a hard pill to swallow or not... it is true! As a realist, I have to be honest with you at all times. How we interact with others and within many of our relationships, whether it is romantic, familial, or professional, have similar elements that may be healthy or unhealthy. How you handle relationships from your childhood says a lot about how you will handle them as an adult and what you will pass down to future generations.

There are typically three ways this dynamic plays out in our lives.

1. Growing up, both your parents showed you what a healthy relationship looks like. There was love, respect, and good communication skills displayed regularly.

2. You did not have the best examples of what a parental relationship or healthy relationship looked like. Your parents may have gotten divorced while you were young like mine did or they were never together in a formal relationship. You saw unresolved conflict modeled through domestic violence, criticism, judgment, name-calling, ultimatums, silent treatment, defensiveness, and threats.

   Let me throw you a little curveball; some of your parents stayed together and still exhibited some, if not all, of those behaviors. Just because two people stay together does not make their relationship healthier than those who decide to separate. While working with thousands of couples, I have seen two of the most toxic people decide to stay together and think they are helping their children; in reality, they are doing themselves, their children, and the next generation a massive disservice.

If you grew up in the second scenario, chances are you try your best to be the exact opposite of who your parents were and what they did. It is not always what your parents did, but also what they did not do that provided an example. Striving to be different from them is perfectly fine because it should yield different outcomes. The different outcomes can transcend generations and put your lineage on a better track toward healthy relationships. All it takes is one person to do something different in your family.

Will you be that one?

3. Your parents weren't the best example, like in the second scenario, but you find yourself being just like them even as you try to be different from

them. I know that sounds horrible, but it is not easy to undo things that have been embedded in you from childhood. We cannot unsee what we have seen, and we cannot undo what was done to us. The past is the past. It is all about how you manage it and how it affects your life moving forward.

Some of the behaviors and patterns from our childhood do not have to be massive or damaging.

As I have gotten older, I have realized that there are qualities and characteristics my parents exemplified that I want to uphold, and those are values that I want to instill in my own family. However, there are other qualities and poor examples that I want to stay away from and not pass down to my future generations. There are good things that I want to pull towards me and bad things I would rather push away. I can acknowledge that no matter how much I try, it often feels like the good, bad, and in between are deeply embedded in me.

For example, my older sister made me realize I was saying and doing the exact things that my mom said and did. It was almost like it was embedded in my DNA, and I could not get away from it.

Regardless of how you were raised: a healthy environment, a semi-healthy environment, or a completely toxic environment, we have consciously and unconsciously instilled ideas of how we should handle relationships, no matter their capacity. In reality, you either handle relationships positively or negatively. Period. Ultimately, our relationships with our children, strangers, co-workers, family, and friends are all impacted by our childhood experiences. These relationships are essential to our lives, and we can't get away from them, no matter how hard we try, so we should work to ensure they are as healthy and harmonious as possible.

Take a moment to think about your childhood and those who raised you. Don't judge whatever thoughts come to mind but notice if what you recall is more positive or negative.

Write down how your upbringing has impacted how you deal with others today.

_____

_____

_____

_____

_____

_____

_____

_____

_____

_____

_____

_____

_____

_____

_____

_____

_____

_____

_____

_____

_____

_____

Hard Work or Harmony?

_____

_____

_____

_____

_____

_____

_____

_____

_____

_____

_____

_____

What are some things you want to change?

Hard Work or Harmony?

_____

_____

_____

_____

_____

_____

_____

_____

_____

_____

_____

_____

_____

_____

_____

_____

_____

_____

_____

_____

_____

_____

_____

_____

_____

_____

_____

_____

_____

_____

_____

_____

_____

What do you want to keep the same? Why?

_____

_____

_____

_____

_____

_____

_____

_____

_____

_____

_____

_____

_____

_____

_____

_____

_____

_____

_____

_____

_____

_____

_____

_____

_____

_____

_____

_____

_____

_____

Hard Work or Harmony?

_____

_____

_____

_____

_____

_____

_____

_____

_____

_____

_____

_____

_____

_____

_____

_____

_____

Chapter 2
THE RELEVANCE OF RELATIONSHIPS

It is beautiful that relationships are essential, and they are necessary. Once we realize that we can't do everything on our own and can't do everything ourselves, we learn to appreciate why relationships of all kinds are of the utmost importance. God created us to have two-dimensional relational experiences: vertical and horizontal. Although this is not meant to be a spiritual lesson, there are some fundamental principles I want to help you understand. The vertical relational experience speaks to being connected with the creator, which speaks directly to who we are, why we were created, our purpose on this earth, what we desire, our wants, and our needs. Knowing there is something bigger than you that orchestrates your being and our world and connecting to that source is the driving force to oneness and harmony. That's a vertical relationship, up and down.

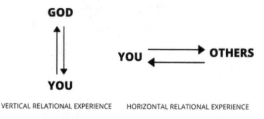

VERTICAL RELATIONAL EXPERIENCE   HORIZONTAL RELATIONAL EXPERIENCE

The horizontal relational experience is across-- that is you and me, it is not always about God and us. It's also about how we connect with the people He has placed in our lives. Those people can be your mom, dad, cousin, boss at work, children, friends, and strangers. We can't rely on only one relational experience to show and guide us on how we're supposed to experience life. We cannot rely solely on people, nor can we rely solely on God's relationship to magically do everything for us.

In the vertical and horizontal relational experience, God requires us to do the work. It would be great if He were like a genie from Aladdin, and everything that we desired and wanted would be granted to us. If we could rub the magic lamp, break out in song, get three wishes, and all of them would come true, then (boom!) our lives would be perfect. But life doesn't happen that way, and God requires us to have an intentional relational experience with Him. That means He requires us to do the work, often first. Faith without works is dead.

When we want to have a healthy dynamic or relationship with someone outside of ourselves, God doesn't magically do it. He requires us to put in the work so that He can bless it and work it out. He requires us to seek answers through prayer, meditation, and communion.

When we want something, we often petition, "God, please make this happen. Please give me a job. Please allow me to get pregnant because I've been struggling for years. Please allow my business to grow and be amazing. Please develop my friendships and send people to me who genuinely want to see me succeed and not just want something from me. Please help me with money because I do not know how I will pay my rent this month." It's okay to send those prayers up to God; however, He often delivers the answers to those prayers through another person.

To get an answered prayer, we have to seek out others. For example, if I ask God to help me pay my rent because I am short this month, instead of $100 magically popping up in my wallet, God may place me on my neighbor's heart. The neighbor does not know why, but he has a strong desire to give me money without me asking or telling them about my need. I receive the money, and in return, my neighbor and I become the friends that neither of us knew we needed. God answered the prayer of the need while giving me the bonus of a great friend.

How about this one? Have you ever been going about your week as usual when someone you haven't talked to in a long time pops up in your head? You decide to reach out to that person and find out the person is going through a tough time, and they were praying for a friend. God used you to fill a relational void for someone else. We often underestimate the power of those urges; however, they are the ties that bind us together. Whether we are providing for someone else or receiving a blessing from someone else, these connections can be God working through us to strengthen our horizontal relationships.

To Love and Be Loved

We are wired and created to love and be loved. It is the essence of why we are on this earth. No matter how many individuals and couples I work with, at the core, their ultimate desire is always to love and be loved. If one of our core desires is to love, we should be giving that gift away freely. If the other core value is to be loved, then we have to receive it when it comes. It shouldn't be based on conditions. My love for you shouldn't be based on what you've done for me. No, no, no, no, no! That is wrong. Giving love and being loved is reciprocity. If you want love, you have to give it. You cannot get something you are unwilling to give.

According to FTD.com, the eight different types of love are:

1. **Philia** (Affectionate Love) - A love that runs deep in true friendships

2. **Pragma** (Enduring Love) - Mature love that develops over time

3. **Storge** (Familiar Love) - Flows between parents and children or childhood friends

4. **Eros** (Romantic Love) - Personal infatuation and physical pleasure

5. **Ludus** (Playful Love) - Flirting and beginning stages of intimate love

6. **Mania** (Obsessive Love) - Obsessiveness or madness over a love partner

7. **Philautia** (Self-Love) - Having a healthy love towards oneself (self-compassion)

8. **Agape** (Selfless Love) - An empathetic attitude of love towards everyone and anyone

As you can see, there are so many different types of loves. No matter how you feel on any given day, God requires us to love and connect with other people. Some people are hermits, introverts, homebodies, or have mental health issues and do not desire to connect with other people. However, if you think about it, you can rarely go a full day without connecting with at least ONE person. You may get a text message that requires a response. You may get an email regarding something important. A stranger might accidentally call your cell phone, and you answer. While at the gas station, you might interact with the clerk. You may go into the grocery store and have to ask for assistance. You may see a homeless person on the street and exchange hellos. Those are interactions. They may be minimal; they may not be on a grand scale, but those interactions are ways that we connect with people regularly, and we don't think twice about them. We connect with others because it is essential to our livelihood.

Can you imagine going days or weeks without interacting with anyone? Sometimes it is good to retreat and spend time alone. There is nothing wrong with much-needed self-care, a solo trip, or a spa day. I'm all for that. But most of the time, those things don't provide us the same long-term fulfillment as togetherness.

According to a discussion by St. Paul's Collegiate School Hamilton, in 1944, an experiment was conducted in the United States on 40 newborn infants to determine whether individuals could thrive alone on basic physiological needs without affection. This was before law and ethics became an important factor in tests and experiments. Twenty newborn infants were housed in a special facility where they had caregivers who would go in to feed them, bathe them, and change their diapers, but they would do nothing else. The caregivers were instructed not to look at or touch the babies more than necessary and to never communicate with them. All their physical needs were attended to scrupulously, and the environment was kept sterile to prevent the babies from becoming ill.

The experiment was halted after four months, by which time, at least half of the babies had died. At least two more died after being rescued and brought into a more natural familial environment. There was no physiological cause for the babies' deaths; they were all physically very healthy. Before each baby died, there was a period where they stopped verbalizing and trying to engage with their caregivers. They stopped moving, crying, or even changing their expression with death following shortly. The babies who had "given up" before being rescued died in the same manner, even though they had been removed from the experimental conditions. While this was taking place, the second group of twenty newborn infants were raised in a separate facility with all their basic physiological needs provided in addition to receiving affection from the caregivers. This time, the outcome was as expected, no deaths occurred. The conclusion was that nurturing is a vital need in humans.

Even at birth, at the first entrance to this world, we connect with other people, and it serves our soul well. It makes us healthy and creates a bond like none other. It's essential to have relationships of all kinds in your life. You can't always pick and choose which relationships you want to have. When was the last time you heard of someone picking their biological parents or choosing who their siblings would be? It does not work that way because God gives you what is necessary and needed.

What is your vertical relationship like with God?

_____

_____

_____

_____

_____

_____

_____

_____

_____

_____

_____

_____

_____

_____

_____

Hard Work or Harmony?

_____

_____

_____

_____

_____

_____

_____

_____

_____

_____

_____

_____

_____

_____

_____

_____

_____

_____

_____

_____

_____

_____

_____

_____

_____

_____

_____

_____

_____

_____

_____

_____

_____

_____

How have your horizontal relationships shaped who you are today?

_____

_____

_____

_____

_____

_____

_____

_____

_____

_____

_____

_____

_____

_____

_____

_____

_____

_____

_____

_____

_____

_____

_____

_____

_____

_____

_____

_____

_____

_____

Hard Work or Harmony?

_____

_____

_____

_____

_____

_____

_____

_____

_____

_____

_____

_____

_____

_____

_____

_____

_____

What is one epiphany you had after reading this chapter about why you need relationships?

_____

_____

_____

_____

_____

_____

_____

_____

_____

_____

_____

_____

_____

_____

Hard Work or Harmony?

_____

_____

_____

_____

_____

_____

_____

_____

_____

_____

_____

_____

_____

_____

_____

_____

_____

_____

_____

_____

_____

_____

_____

_____

_____

_____

_____

_____

_____

_____

_____

_____

_____

_____

Chapter 3
HEALED PEOPLE HAVE HEALTHY CONNECTIONS

B y now, you may be saying, "Yes, Kiaundra. I understand the different types of interpersonal relationships, why we need them, and why it's important. But what is a healthy, harmonious relationship?"

I'm glad you asked because relationships and our perception of a healthy relationship come from our own personal experiences. There are key indicators that help you realize what a healthy relationship should entail. Healthy interpersonal relationships are about mutuality, two or more people developing a relationship of reciprocity. That means I'm giving you something and you're giving me something too. Isn't this concept essential to what we already discussed in Chapter 2, desiring to love and be loved? The same is true for healthy interpersonal relationships. They should not be one-sided, nor should they be off-kilter or unbalanced. They should pull out the best qualities in you every single time. Don't get me wrong; all relationships will not be perfect all of the time. That is unrealistic.

We will discuss the signs of an unhealthy relationship and how to distinguish between an unhealthy relationship and a difficult one. However, sharing essential qualities about who you are and receiving essential qualities about who they are should be a regular conversation. We will breakdown these essential qualities and components in the next chapter.

Reciprocity in relationships should be a universal law. Even if you think some relationships are unequal or lopsided, there is still reciprocity. Think about an infant child and its caregiver, even that relationship has an exchange. Newborn babies give you joy (or at least they should in most cases). A baby who is totally dependent on its caregiver for their livelihood, food, clothes, to be cleaned up from its poopy diapers, for learning, hugs, and kisses--even those infants give their caregiver something. They provide them with joy and happiness. You have to be a cold-hearted individual to see a cute baby, and it not at least make you smile. If something so small who can't do anything for you can still provide you with some essential happiness, can you imagine how much more healthy, adult relationships should add to your life?

If you find yourself giving, giving, and giving some more but not receiving back an ounce of what you are giving, it's time to reevaluate that relationship. The people you are connected with should be pulling out the best qualities in you. Suppose you're realizing that you're having negative thoughts and emotions such as always being mad, angry, agitated, annoyed, or confused when you are around certain people. In that case, I encourage you to reevaluate those relationships because they are NOT pulling out the best qualities in you; they're pulling out the worst in you. How can you go into the world being great and effective at what you are called to do when those bad qualities are being pulled out of you by those around you?

I am not saying that you can blame others when you feel negative emotions or are not feeling your best. No! That is not what I am saying at all. There is and will always be a level of personal accountability for yourself and your actions. You cannot go through life blaming others for the things you should take responsibility for and expect to receive sympathy. You should take an internal temperature of yourself when you are around your family, friends, romantic interests, and co-workers. Notice how you behave, what you say, what thoughts pop into your head, and your mood.

If your interpersonal connections are not based on an even exchange, they will fail. I know you're probably wondering what an unhealthy relationship looks like? Don't worry. I got you. I will give you multiple examples and tangible components for your reference; however, you have to stick with me a bit longer. Providing this groundwork is essential to the other concepts in this book to making sense and coming alive.

Healthy interpersonal relationships are not based on the qualities we often think. They are not based on blood, nor are they based on time, culture, sexual orientation, religious affiliation, race, age, or ethnicity. None of those factors matter when it comes to relationships. For example, have you ever became close with someone you just met, and you're closer to them than someone you have known for years? That's because time doesn't determine the health of a relationship.

Have you had an auntie, uncle, or "play cousin" who you are not blood-related to, but you have known them for so long they've been incorporated into your family? They feel like a blood relative, they treat you like a blood relative, and you all don't even question that you are not biologically related. That's an example of how healthy relationships are not contingent on blood.

The same goes for the other factors such as race, age, ethnicity, religious preference, sexual orientation, or culture. I have friends who are 15 or more years older than me, and we get along exceptionally well. I get along with them better than some of my friends in my age group. The same applies to race and ethnicity. I have friends who are not of African American descent, and we are the closest of friends. Things that we think matter aren't always as important as we imagine.

I want you to reevaluate all of the relationships in your life to determine what they are based on. Are they based on the time you have known each other, a common sexual orientation, or your shared religious beliefs? What about those people who don't fit into a category of sameness? We don't discount those relationships and say, "Oh, we can't be cool because you're different from me." Those differences often breed the closest, healthiest interactions I've ever seen.

Think about the following questions to get your mental juices flowing about the different interpersonal relationships in your life.

How do you feel when you are around your family?

_____

_____

_____

_____

_____

_____

_____

_____

_____

_____

_____

_____

_____

_____

Hard Work or Harmony?

_____

_____

_____

_____

_____

_____

_____

_____

_____

_____

_____

_____

_____

_____

_____

_____

_____

_____

_____

_____

_____

_____

_____

_____

_____

_____

_____

_____

_____

_____

_____

_____

_____

What typically goes through your mind when you are around your co-workers?

_____

_____

_____

_____

_____

_____

_____

_____

_____

_____

_____

_____

_____

_____

Hard Work or Harmony?

_____

_____

_____

_____

_____

_____

_____

_____

_____

_____

_____

_____

_____

_____

_____

_____

_____

How do you behave when you are with your
friends?

_____

_____

_____

_____

_____

_____

_____

_____

_____

_____

_____

_____

_____

Hard Work or Harmony?

_____

_____

_____

_____

_____

_____

_____

_____

_____

_____

_____

_____

_____

_____

_____

_____

_____

_____

_____

_____

_____

_____

_____

_____

_____

_____

_____

_____

_____

_____

_____

_____

_____

_____

Chapter 4
HARMONY IS THE RESULT OF HEALTHY RELATIONSHIPS

Y ou are probably wondering what a healthy interpersonal relationship entails. You may be saying to yourself that we talked A LOT about reciprocity, and now, you want to know about the qualities you are supposed to reciprocate. There are seven key components that every relationship needs to thrive. As we go through the seven elements, think about how they relate to your relationships, if you have them, and how you can apply them if you don't.

These components are essential to every healthy relationship, but if you do not have all of them, you can develop them as long as both parties are willing to work on the process. If you have them all and your relationships are perfect, then there is no reason to read this book. Just kidding! That means your goal is to keep and maintain those relationships no matter which season of life you are in. If you're missing a few, you can develop them now that you know what they are.

#1 Trust

Most people fall into one of two categories. In the first category, your relationships begin with all the trust in the world. You believe that people should be trusted until they do something wrong--you trust them with everything in your being. The second category is when you start without any trust. You believe that trust should be earned and not freely given. In this scenario, trust can take a long time to build, but it can also be snatched away in a moment. No matter which school of thought you come from regarding trust, it is one of the hardest things to rebuild once broken because it involves forgiveness. A healthy connection with family, friends, and co-workers is nothing without trust.

EXTRA TIP: To be trusted, you need to be trustworthy. Work to embody the traits you seek in others. If you are trustworthy, you will attract people who you can trust, right? If you are a shady person and no one can trust you because you lack integrity, you cannot wonder why everyone around you cannot be trusted. Hold the mirror up to yourself. When you exemplify a particular quality, that quality oozes out of you, and it attracts those who are similar.

#2 Support

Support is a huge one! Support means that there should be ways that you show up emotionally and physically in the relationship to let the other person know you have their back. It is one thing to say you support someone, but do you show it? Don't forget encouragement and kind words are just as important as physically showing up for a loved one at their event, show, awards ceremony, graduation, or sports game.

Supporting one another can manifest in many different forms. It may be a text message to say how proud you are, a quick phone call to say you will show up, a gift because you cannot physically be there, sharing or posting their product or service on social media, or you may buy something they are selling. If your relationships are not supportive, you are missing one of the essential qualities of a healthy relationship.

EXTRA TIP: You do not always have to AGREE with the other person to support them. If you love and care about them, you realize they are on their own journey, and you will be there to provide emotional or physical support, if needed. For example, you may not like the person your best friend is in a romantic relationship with because you think that person is not right for them. But if they were to break up, you should still show up to console him/her. You do not throw it in their face saying, "See, I told you that fool was no good for you!"

#3 Cooperation

This one is simple, right? It's the willingness to be on the same team and put in the necessary work towards a common goal. Remember, we are not just talking about romantic relationships. We're talking about ALL relationships - relationships at work, relationships in business, and relationships with family and friends. You should be on the same team working towards the same goal. If you guys are opponents and fighting each other while on the same team, then guess what? No one is going to win!

EXTRA TIP: Cooperation is a drama-free zone. Do you have time for drama? Because I know I don't. All drama does is make you upset and pull you further away from your intended goal, which will take you even longer to reach it. Keep that in mind when working on your interpersonal relationships.

#4 Safety

Safety is when you are free and protected from any physical, emotional, and verbal abuse between individuals or a group of people. Physical, emotional, and verbal abuse are real. If you feel unsafe at any time, give yourself permission to remove yourself from the situation, no matter what type of relationship it is. It can be a parent, sibling, stranger, cousin, uncle, boss, business partner, mentor, family friend, politician, or a clergyperson. You deserve to be safe at all times!

I want to repeat that for the people who are having difficulty digesting this one. You deserve to be safe at all times!

EXTRA TIP: It doesn't matter where you were, what you did, what you looked like, what you had on or what you said; you deserved to be emotionally, spiritually, physically, and financially safe.

#5 Honesty

Honesty is one of my favorite elements because I grew up in Compton, where honesty was everything. You can't be honest without speaking truthful words. We would say, "my word is bond." That means "I am telling the truth," or "You can trust what I just said." If your words do not have integrity, then guess what? You have nothing. Always tell the truth. No one likes a liar, and no one wants to be lied to. Whether it's your past, present, or future, be honest about what you have gone through, what you are currently experiencing and any issues that you foresee arising in the near future. This is all about integrity and character.

One of the four agreements written by Don Miguel Ruiz is to be impeccable with your word. He states, "Speak with integrity. Say only what you mean. Avoid using the words to speak against yourself or to gossip about others. Use the power of your word in the direction of truth and love."

EXTRA TIP: When a person is not honest, it is a character flaw. It can make someone question everything else about you because you were dishonest about one thing. You do not want to be labeled a liar!

#6 Accountability

Accountability is necessary for growth. It is the space where personal and collective goals are birthed and where the real #RelationshipGoals originated.

#FriendGoals, #BusinessGoals, #FamilyGoals, or whatever else you desire to hashtag is essential to your growth and development. I do not want you to be one of those people who uses hashtags just for the heck of it. I want these #Goals to exemplify your life. We are not fronting and perpetrating on social media; we want our business, family, friends, and work-life to be amazing. You cannot be amazing by yourself. You need someone to hold you to the fire when you don't want to do something. You need someone to remind you of your weight loss goals when you get lazy. You need someone to remind you of your goals when you start doubting whether you should go back to school, when you stop reading 30 minutes a day to further your knowledge, when you get relaxed about finding a new job, learning a new language, starting a business, getting married or starting that family... all of that requires accountability.

Your loved one, whoever it is, should be an accountability partner for you. That means if I say, "Hey! I want to make sure that I work out every single day for one hour, five times a week," that person should help to keep me focused on my goal. Either they will work out with me or check-in by saying, "You said you were going to work out. Did you?"

Accountability is key.

EXTRA TIP: You should be accountable at all times because it is not a one-time, sometime thing; it's an all-the-time thing.

#7 Respect

The last one is probably one of my favorites above honesty, and that is respect.

R-E-S-P-E-C-T

I'm not going to break out in song and say, "Find out what it means to me." I don't want to turn into Aretha Franklin on you all. However, respect is everything in any relationship. Respect is how you think about or treat someone or something.

If you don't have respect, you don't have anything. It is similar to trust. Consider the following when we talk about respect. Is the other person respecting your time, boundaries, goals, money, thoughts, and feelings? If the people you are connected with do not respect any of those things, then guess what? It's time for you to reevaluate the relationship.

EXTRA TIP: Having respect for yourself is just as important as having respect for others. The Novelist, Laurence Sterne stated, "Respect for ourselves guides our morals; respect for others guides our manners."

Those are the seven key components that every interpersonal relationship should have to thrive.

Hard Work or Harmony?

Which of the seven components do you need to work so you can be better in your relationships with others?

_____

_____

_____

_____

_____

_____

_____

_____

_____

_____

_____

_____

_____

_____

_____

_____

_____

_____

_____

_____

_____

_____

_____

_____

_____

_____

_____

_____

_____

Hard Work or Harmony?

_____

_____

_____

_____

_____

_____

_____

_____

_____

_____

_____

_____

_____

_____

_____

_____

_____

Which of the seven components do you need to hold others accountable to in how they treat YOU?

_____

_____

_____

_____

_____

_____

_____

_____

_____

_____

_____

_____

_____

_____

Hard Work or Harmony?

_____

_____

_____

_____

_____

_____

_____

_____

_____

_____

_____

_____

_____

_____

_____

_____

_____

_____

_____

_____

_____

_____

_____

_____

_____

_____

_____

_____

_____

_____

_____

_____

_____

_____

_____

_____

Bonus Chapter
PERSONALITY TYPES AFFECT
PERSONAL RELATIONSHIPS

What would you say if I gave you a better way to understand yourself and those you are in connection with daily? Think about it. Every person on the planet was born with a personality. That means everyone's personality is not the same and comes in many different shapes, sizes, and ways. What if I gave you some tips, keen insight, and some therapeutic advice into your personality and others' personality to help your connections be more successful? What would you say? Well, even if you said "no," I am going to give you this gift because I know it will be a game-changer for you.

There are 16 different personality types. Yes, I said 16 different ones! I know you're probably like, "Oh my goodness, Kiaundra! I have to learn all 16 different types?" I'm not saying that you have to learn these in full detail. I hope you will understand them and consider each for yourself and those you are in relationship with.

Knowing these personality types will help you see how YOU and others manage the huge topics we've discussed thus far. They show strengths and weaknesses, how we show up in romantic relationships, how we manage and maintain friendships, and how we are as parents or parents to be. They show our career paths, what we choose, and why we chose them as well as how we show up in the workplace and what habits we have, whether as a business owner or an employee. They show us so many different things about who we are and how we show up that it's kind of scary to think our complexities can be summed up and broken down into different categories. I have taken this test multiple times, and it continues to be extremely accurate.

I encourage you to take the 16 Personalities Test to learn more about yourself. It's a free online test at www.16personalities.com. When you tap into this free test, you will get the descriptions below of the different types, and you will learn what drives people, inspires them, and worries them. It ultimately helps you to build more meaningful relationships.

You're probably like, "Kiaundra, you've been talking about these 16 personality types. What are they?" I'm going to break them down for you to give you a snapshot. There are four different personality categories: Analysts, Diplomats, Sentinels, and Explorers. Within each category, there are four distinct personality types. Here is a brief overview of each type and a short description of how they show up in the world. Take note of which one(s) may apply to you then take the test to see if you are accurate.

The Analysts

Architect - imaginative and strategic thinkers with a plan for every single thing on the planet

Logician - an innovative inventor with an unquenchable thirst for knowledge

Commander - bold, imaginative, strong-willed leaders, always finding a way or making a way out of something

Debater - smart and curious and they cannot resist an intellectual challenge at all

The Diplomats

Advocate - quiet and mystical, yet very inspiring and a tireless idealist

Mediator - poetic, kind, altruistic. They're always eager to give and to help people for a good cause

Protagonist - a charismatic leader. They're also inspiring and able to mesmerize their listeners at any given time

Campaigner - enthusiastic, creative, social, free-spirited and can always find a reason to smile

The Sentinels

Logistician - practical and fact-minded individuals whose reliability cannot be doubted

Defender - very dedicated and warm protectors always ready to defend their loved ones

Executive - an excellent administrator. They're unsurpassed at managing things or people

Consul - an extraordinarily caring, social, popular person and always eager to help

The Explorers

Virtuoso - bold, practical, experimental, and the master of all kinds of tools

Adventurer - flexible and a charming artist. Always ready to explore and experience something new

Entrepreneur - smart, energetic, very perceptive to people who truly enjoy living on the edge

Entertainer - spontaneous, energetic, enthusiastic people and life is never boring when you are around them

I know this is a quick and abbreviated version, and I'm sure while you were reading these over, you were thinking about who you are and where your loved ones fall into these categories. Go ahead and take the 16 Personalities Test because you will be surprised how accurate it is. You will be sharing this personality test with people in your life to help them understand you more and to get a glimpse into how they manage different areas of their life. It will give you the blueprint on why they are the way they are and why they do the things they do, so you can stop pulling your hair out about how you interact with them.

Another one of my favorite personality quizzes is The Big Five Personality Traits.

Think of the word O-C-E-A-N. OCEAN is the acronym to easily help you remember: **O**penness, **C**onscientiousness, **E**xtraversion, **A**greeableness, and **N**euroticism. According to 123test.com, several independent sets of researchers discovered and defined the five broad traits based on empirical, data-driven research. Human resource professionals often use the Big Five personality dimensions to help place employees because these dimensions are considered the underlying characteristics that make up an individual's overall personality.

- **Openness** - People who like to learn new things and enjoy new experiences usually score high in openness, which includes traits like being insightful, imaginative, and having a wide variety of interests.

- **Conscientiousness** - People that have a high degree of conscientiousness are reliable and prompt. The traits include being organized, methodic, and thorough.

- **Extraversion** - Extraverts get their energy from interacting with others, while introverts get their energy from within themselves. Extraversion traits are energetic, talkative, and assertive.

- **Agreeableness** - These individuals are friendly, cooperative, and compassionate. People with low agreeableness may be more distant. Agreeable traits include being kind, affectionate, and sympathetic.

- **Neuroticism** - Neuroticism is also sometimes called Emotional Stability. This dimension relates to one's emotional stability and degree of negative emotions. People that score high on neuroticism often experience emotional instability and negative emotions. The traits include being moody and tense.

The interesting part of the Big 5 Personality Types is that it is just the beginning. If you take the free test at 123test.com, you will see that each main trait described above gets segmented into six facets in which you score low-high compared to others.

There are many different personality tests and traits, but I wanted to introduce you to these two because they are my favorite, the most simplest, and they will provide you with a deeper understanding of yourself and others.

Chapter 5
HOPING FOR HARMONY

I t is important to understand which of the seven healthy relationship components from Chapter 4 you share with your connections. However, the real question you may be asking is, how do we navigate them? We know that relationships take work. The relationships you have with family, friends, and co-workers are based on filling each other's cups. However, you must be aware that how you like your cup to be filled may be completely different from how the other person likes their cup to be filled. This is why it's important to learn people's love languages. Although we often talk about love languages from the perspective of romantic relationships, they apply to all relationships. If you haven't tapped into Gary Chapman's, The Five Love Languages, you should. He has books on the love languages for romantic relationships, teenagers, children, your relationship with God, military personnel, and even singles.

The 5 Love Languages are: Words of Affirmation, Acts of Service, Receiving Gifts, Quality Time, and Physical Touch.

1. **Words of Affirmation** - This love language expresses love with words. Verbal compliments don't have to be complicated; the shortest and simplest praises can be the most effective.

2. **Acts of Service** - "Actions speak louder than words." This love language expresses itself by doing things that you know the other person would like. Cooking a meal and bringing it over to a co-worker who takes care of her aging par-

ents, helping a friend who just had a baby fold laundry, and picking up a family member's prescription who is ill are all acts of service. They require some thought, time, and effort.

3. **Receiving Gifts** - This love language isn't necessarily materialistic. It just means that a meaningful or thoughtful gift makes the other person feel loved and appreciated. Something as simple as picking up a pint of their favorite ice cream after a long work week can make a huge impact.

4. **Quality Time** - This love language is all about undivided attention, which means no televisions, no smartphones, or other distractions. If this is the other person's primary language, they don't just want to be included during this period; they want to be the center of your attention uninterrupted. They want to spend quality time with you and you only.

5. **Physical Touch** - Nothing is more impactful than the physical touch of another. This does not mean sexual. They feel more connected and safer in a relationship by sitting close, hugging, etc.

Kiaundra Jackson, LMFT

Ultimately, the 5 Love Languages teach us the way we give and receive love is different. You want to make sure you know what other people's love languages are, so you won't treat them how *you* want to treat them versus how *they* desire to be treated. The goal is to feel heard, understood, loved, and to keep your "love tank" full. Think about it. When one feels heard, understood, and loved, there is less drama, tension, and disagreements. That should be enough reason to learn the love languages of those you are most connected with.

I want to scream to the world off the top of a mountain that relationships are NOT hard work. That is absolutely untrue. I want to encourage people to remove from their vocabulary and thought process that relationships are hard work. You're probably a little confused because people say relationships are hard all the time and it is even in the title of this very book. You may not fully agree, but I want you to remove the narrative of relationships being hard work from your mind.

Words are powerful, and our thoughts can create a reality. So, when we think something is hard or difficult (and we say it aloud), it tells our brain we will have to put in too much time and energy. It places our brain in a different perspective and on a different track, resulting in us not being as intentional because it feels beyond our reach or too difficult.

I remember not being good at math. Taking Statistics in high school was like pulling teeth because I could not pass a test to save my life. I convinced myself that it was too hard despite the positive reinforcement my mom tried to give me. She would say, "If you at least get a C, I will take you to Jamba Juice." I loved Jamba Juice (a plant-based smoothie and juicery) at the time, so trust me, I was aiming for the C. However, the C never came because of all of my negative self-talk. I never did better because of my "stinking thinking" about myself and my statistics capabilities.

Here is a concept I teach my clients: Your thoughts affect your feelings. Your feelings affect your behavior. Your behavior affects your results and outcome.

If we switch our mindset to think, "the relationships we have with our family, friends, and co-workers are manageable, we can get through this, we're going to get through anything." We will put more time, energy, and effort into something we are willing to fight for versus thinking that it's hard. Feeling confident and having positive affirmations that relationships do *take work*, but it's not always *hard work* puts our mind at ease.

Instead of thinking your relationships are hard, think of them as harmonious. Here goes that word again, lol. When I think of harmony, I think of the Ancient Chinese Philosophy of dualism: Yin Yang. It is described as seemingly opposite or contrary forces potentially being complementary and interdependent as they relate to one another. Because no two people are alike, it is unrealistic to expect the person we have a relationship with will be like us nor is it realistic to expect any two of our relationships will be alike. When we accept these factors and look for ways to complement each other, then we are able to develop healthy relationships that are interdependent and balanced.

The goal is to pace yourself in your relationships based on your personal values. There will be periods and timeframes in a relationship where you should have markers of progress with those you are connected with, and there should be some traction you can tangibly note. If you are in an interpersonal relationship with your mom, your children, or at work and find yourself in the same space with them that you were five years ago, then the relationship is not progressing.

It could be a values clash. The things you value, the core values of self, may not translate well to the core values of what the other person embodies. There is a collision happening that is preventing you from putting one step in front of the other to show the relationship is progressing over time.

Think about it. When you notice things are not moving forward, there is typically a problem. Just like in a romantic relationship, there should be markers of progress. If you are taking the more traditional route, you should be dating, getting to know each other, then becoming exclusive. You should move

94

from exclusivity to being in a relationship to engagement, potentially marriage, and then having children. The advancement of your relationship stages is considered markers of progress. If you have been in the dating phase for the last ten years, honey, there is no progress! Having progress in your interpersonal relationships is key to navigating and managing them successfully.

The question I get asked most often is, do healthy relationships run their course? Meaning, can a relationship be good, then it's kind of like we're just not on the same page anymore, and we're going our separate ways. I want to encourage people and provide a thorough understanding that ANY relationship can run its course. Even healthy relationships can run their course. It doesn't always have to be toxic or unhealthy because people sometimes drift apart. Often when a relationship ends, it's not on good terms and can be very unhealthy. Sometimes it's nasty; it's an argument; a verbal fight, or even a physical fight. It could involve issues with children and custody agreements. It can literally go left really quick. In the words of Drake, it can go from "0 to 100 real quick."

I don't think most people have a good model of how to end a relationship in a healthy manner.

When was the last time you sat down with somebody you no longer wanted to connect with and said, "Hey, you know what? I feel like we've run our race. We're not really connecting that much anymore. I wish we wouldn't be friends." Those conversations are rare. However, I think it is an amazing and mature thing to do, but it's so very rare because we don't know how to end things well.

We are in this cutoff and block culture of, if I no longer want to be friends with you, I'm going to stop talking to you, stop responding to your text messages, phone calls, emails, and I might even block you on social media or via text where you can't call, text, or email me ever again. You have no way to get in contact with me. That has become our norm and our go-to, but we need to learn and evolve with a different skillset.

I cannot tell you how many times clients have ghosted me. Yes, I have been ghosted by clients who stop coming to their counseling sessions and never return phone calls or emails. No matter how much progress we have made, I do not take it personally. It is a candid reminder that people would rather avoid a small conversation than address any potential issues head-on.

Managing relationships is a skillset. You have to learn how to have healthy relationships with others just like you learned a craft in school, got a degree, or learned to play a sport or an instrument; you have to learn, study, and practice. For some reason, we don't think of relationships in that aspect, but I'm encouraging you to think about things differently.

Reflection: Let go of the people, places, and things that no longer serve you. Make room for the things that are meant to be in your life long-term. Are there any relationships in your life that have run their course?

_____

_____

_____

_____

_____

_____

_____

_____

_____

_____

_____

_____

_____

_____

_____

_____

_____

_____

_____

_____

_____

_____

_____

_____

_____

_____

_____

_____

Hard Work or Harmony?

_____

_____

_____

_____

_____

_____

_____

_____

_____

_____

_____

_____

_____

_____

_____

_____

_____

_____

How can you end those relationships gracefully?

_____

_____

_____

_____

_____

_____

_____

_____

_____

_____

_____

_____

_____

_____

Hard Work or Harmony?

_____

_____

_____

_____

_____

_____

_____

_____

_____

_____

_____

_____

_____

_____

_____

_____

_____

Bonus Chapter
RELATIONSHIP RULES FOR
INTROVERTS AND EXTROVERTS

S ome things in life are absolutely, positively, crystal clear like eye color, real hair color, and how tall or short someone is. Then, there are instinctual drives inside us that contribute to our personality and how we show up in the world. A lot of you have probably heard the terms introverts and extroverts. Let's break down the difference between the two to help you understand how introverts and extroverts show up in the world and how this can be positively or negatively impacting your interactions.

Extroverts are more outgoing, talkative people, while introverts are quieter and more reserved. I like to think about extroversion and introversion in its simplest terms. Extroversion focuses on the outside world, meaning they get all of their energy from being around people. Introversion is the opposite. They focus on the inner self and get all of their energy from being alone, quieter, thoughtful, and more reserved.

According to 16personalities.com, an:

Introvert personality = STRENGTH IN RESERVE

Extrovert personality = POWER OF ENGAGEMENT

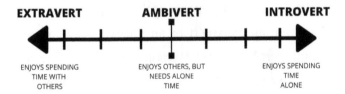

I've had people ask me if there is a way to change from being an extrovert to an introvert or vice versa. I think about extroversion and introversion as a continuum. It's like a 12-inch ruler; on one end is extroversion, and on the other end is introversion with many different skills in between. You don't typically fit neatly into one category.

People in the middle are considered ambiverts; they have mastered being between both at any given time. The person exhibits introversion and extroversion qualities depending on their mood, context, goals, who they are around, and their location. Understanding that you can't always fit into these nice little boxes is important when dealing with extroversion and introversion.

If you're doing internal reflections, ask yourself if you are an extrovert or an introvert? Or are you an ambivert? This understanding will determine how you show up in other people's lives and how they view you. There is no right or wrong way. Introverts are not better than extroverts, extroverts are not better than introverts, and being an ambivert is not a superpower because they can do both. However, being aware of the difference helps you understand where you get the most of your energy.

If you're an extrovert, you can be the life of the party. You can walk into a social gathering, a party, a networking event for professionals, or a family gathering, and you're able to talk to everybody and "work the room." You get to know people, have drinks, and laugh while meeting people easily and having a wonderful time.

But if we take that same scenario and insert an introvert, they may have a completely different experience. They may not want to go to the event at all or walk into the scenario and not feel the same because they're not as social. They may sit in a corner by themselves and not talk to anyone. They may briefly say hello to people but find one or two people to cling to and talk to for the whole night. They're not a social butterfly. They may be the designated driver and feel very uncomfortable, or they may choose to leave the function early, depending on how much energy they felt that they've expended.

I know many introverts in my personal life, and they have shared that it is physically and emotionally draining when they go to social gatherings or events. They either didn't want to go in the first place or knew that they would have to turn on a little bit of their extroversion so they will not seem "awkward." These same individuals say they have to "recover" after dishing out the energy they had to muster up to seem social. They may require additional days following an event to refuel.

Since the three types are on a continuum, you may not fall into any category perfectly. You may even be thinking, "I am an introvert, but I am not that extreme." That is okay. Remember, everyone handles their introversion and extroversion differently because no two people are the same.

I feel like I can relate to both of these in a very interesting way. I believe I am an ambivert who can navigate between the two.

As a licensed therapist, I talk to people all the time. As a television personality, I am in front of thousands and even millions on any given day. As an award-winning speaker and bestselling author, I stand on stages in front of hundreds to share words to transform lives on a massive scale. Can you imagine how much energy and extroversion it takes for me to do even ONE of those tasks? I remember very early in my career; I was still trying to figure out how I wanted to show up in the world and navigate this space. I kept finding myself drained after I would get off of stages. I would do my keynote speech to empower, impact, and change lives; then, I would get off stage, sell books, talk to people, answer their relationship questions, and take selfies.

I would do all of that; then, people would ask, "Hey Kiaundra, let's go out to dinner. Let's go out for drinks. Let's continue the night." I had to tell them no because I felt so tired. I was physically and emotionally drained. All I wanted to do was be by myself to refuel and recharge. That is an example of how I can turn on the extroversion for different scenarios, moods, places, and goals. What people don't realize is that I absolutely love being by myself. I know that might sound weird to someone who's always in the forefront, but I value my alone time, my thoughts, quietness, and being by myself. There have been times when I have literally turned off the radio in my car or turned off the television because I wanted to be with my thoughts and didn't want to have anything else coming into my consciousness.

That's when I learned I was dead smack in the middle of the continuum. I can do both, although I am unsure if that's a gift or a curse. No matter which category you find yourself in extroversion, introversion, or ambiversion, you are perfectly fine the way that you are. You will find people you gel well with because they are the same as you, or you may click with someone who is the complete opposite. I've been able to find people of different personality types that have shifted and changed how I view myself and how I show up for other people. This understanding allows us to give people a little more grace when we know which category they fall into, right?

If they're an introvert, they may be extremely private or extremely shy. It's not our responsibility to push them into a social gathering, make them attend events with us, or encourage them to talk to groups of people because that might be too much for them. We have to be respectful of what someone chooses to do and not judge them based on how they want to interact and govern their lives. No matter which category you find yourself in, remember you are valued exactly the way you are, and there should be no one or nothing that can make you change that. No matter what the world may say, no matter how many people are trying to encourage you to do something differently, you are the way you are for a reason. Operate in that authentically.

Dr. Seuss said it best "Today you are you, that is truer than true. There is no one alive who is youer than YOU!"

Where do you fall in the continuum of introversion, extraversion, ambiversion?

_____

_____

_____

_____

_____

_____

_____

_____

_____

_____

_____

_____

_____

_____

_____

_____

_____

_____

_____

_____

_____

_____

_____

_____

_____

_____

_____

_____

_____

Hard Work or Harmony?

_____

_____

_____

_____

_____

_____

_____

_____

_____

_____

_____

_____

_____

_____

_____

_____

_____

Do you consider yourself more of an introvert, extrovert, or ambivert?

_____

_____

_____

_____

_____

_____

_____

_____

_____

_____

_____

_____

_____

Hard Work or Harmony?

_____

_____

_____

_____

_____

_____

_____

_____

_____

_____

_____

_____

_____

_____

_____

_____

_____

_____

_____

_____

_____

_____

_____

_____

_____

_____

_____

_____

_____

_____

_____

_____

_____

How does that impact how you interact with your family, friends, and co-workers?

_____

_____

_____

_____

_____

_____

_____

_____

_____

_____

_____

_____

_____

Hard Work or Harmony?

_____

_____

_____

_____

_____

_____

_____

_____

_____

_____

_____

_____

_____

_____

_____

_____

_____

How do others treat you?

_____

_____

_____

_____

_____

_____

_____

_____

_____

_____

_____

_____

_____

_____

_____

Hard Work or Harmony?

Chapter 6
WHEN BOUNDARIES ARE BLURRED

B oundaries are one of the most important aspects of your relationships. Boundaries are invisible lines that we set for ourselves and others. They tell others how to treat us and set rules to be reinforced consistently. Boundaries do not always feel good, and others do not always follow them. There will be some people who will push the limits to find out the consequences of their actions. Boundaries can cause you to end relationships with family, friends, and co-workers who do not respect you.

When we don't end relationships in a healthy way, it leads to unhealthy, unwanted contacts and often toxic ones. Just because a relationship was great when it started, doesn't mean it can't become toxic over time. Just because a relationship didn't start well or started a little rocky doesn't mean that it can't transform and become healthy. The key is for all parties involved to put in the time and energy to make sure the relationship is on the same trajectory.

Here is a list of some signs that you may be in an unhealthy relationship with loved ones.

✗ **When one person projects bad energy onto you all or the majority of the time**

They're constantly like, "Well, I thought that you were this, and I feel like you were that, and I feel like you looked at me wrong and gave me bad vibes." That is not healthy.

✗ **When there is no reciprocity**

We talked about this in the earlier chapters, and what a healthy relationship entails, but when there's no reciprocity in the seven key areas (trust, safety, honesty, respect, accountability, support, cooperation), that can be an unhealthy, unbalanced situation.

✗ When there's a lack of harmony

When you are operating from a place of harmony, (I love to use the word harmony instead of balance) you understand that certain things take priority in certain seasons over other things. You understand if someone is in school and trying to pursue a higher education, they may not be worried about cleaning up and cooking because they're trying to study to set themselves up to do some amazing things in the future. Their priorities are temporarily different.

An example for a romantic relationship would be understanding there will be seasons where everyone may not want to or be able to give 100%. That should be both parties' goals at all times, but it is incredibly unrealistic to think both parties will always give 100%.

The 50/50 rule does not work well, and I do not believe in it because it is ridiculous. In a marriage or a committed relationship, you understand there will be times when you can only give 80%, and the other person will have to pick up the 20%. You may give 10% in another season because you just had a baby and might be experiencing postpartum. You might not be working, and your partner will have to "pick up the slack" and temporarily provide the 90%. We must understand seasons change, but the goal should be to maintain reciprocity and harmony. If there's a lack of harmony, it is an indication of an unhealthy relationship.

✘ When it becomes abusive

If someone is physically, verbally, emotionally, spiritually, or financially abusive to you, it is another indicator of an unhealthy relationship, and you should be considering ways to exit stage left.

✘ When you feel like you're losing yourself

Losing yourself doesn't always have to be about the other person; it could be personal changes you are making, whether conscious or subconscious, as an attempt to please the other person. If you feel like you're losing yourself in a relationship, you're changing who you are, you don't like the same things anymore, you're morphing into another person, or you're losing the things that once brought you joy-- that's an indicator that someone is sucking the life out of you. It is an indicator they no longer desire you to be you and want you to change into someone else.

✗ When boundaries are crossed

If we don't respect our own boundaries, no one else is going to! If someone is continuously crossing your boundaries: physical, emotional, financial, or your time, you should consider this may be an unhealthy relationship. You should also reflect on why you have allowed them to cross your boundaries in the first place.

✗ When there is only one-way communication

We haven't talked extensively about communication in this book because it will be detailed in my upcoming book. Communication needs to be two-way. Yes, you heard me! TWO-WAY. That's why we call it effective two-way communication because if it's only one-sided, then it isn't communication at all. That is one person talking at you, not with you or to you.

✗ When there's more negativity than positivity

When there's more criticism or control than positivity and uplifting behavior, you are in a negative relationship. If you find someone is criticizing you, "Ooh, you do not look good today, honey, I do not like that dress that you have on, your hair is not cute. I need for you to be in the house by eight o'clock today."; that is not uplifting, encouraging, or motivating.

The ultimate test is if the bad outweighs the good. If you can look at the relationship and say the bad outweighs the good, then this may be a person you want to pull back from.

✗ When you are feeling unsafe

Any time that you're unsafe physically, emotionally, financially, or spiritually in the relationship it is not okay and could be a long-term detriment if it's not handled appropriately.

Reflection: Do any of the signs of an unhealthy relationship pertain to your connections with family, friends, or co-workers?

_____

_____

_____

_____

_____

_____

_____

_____

_____

_____

_____

_____

_____

Kiaundra Jackson, LMFT

_____

_____

_____

_____

_____

_____

_____

_____

_____

_____

_____

_____

_____

_____

_____

_____

_____

Hard Work or Harmony?

_____

_____

_____

_____

_____

_____

_____

_____

_____

_____

_____

_____

_____

_____

_____

_____

_____

_____

What are the indicators?

_____

_____

_____

_____

_____

_____

_____

_____

_____

_____

_____

_____

_____

_____

_____

_____

Hard Work or Harmony?

_____

_____

_____

_____

_____

_____

_____

_____

_____

_____

_____

_____

_____

_____

_____

_____

_____

_____

How will you proceed with these relationships moving forward now that you are aware?

_____

_____

_____

_____

_____

_____

_____

_____

_____

_____

_____

_____

_____

Hard Work or Harmony?

_____

_____

_____

_____

_____

_____

_____

_____

_____

_____

_____

_____

_____

_____

_____

_____

_____

Chapter 7
DIFFICULT OR
DEAD-END

Don't get me wrong here! There is a huge difference between an unhealthy relationship and a difficult season with someone you care about. When there is someone in your life who is going through a difficult season, it can look very different. A difficult season can be when someone passes away, a job loss, dealing with medical or health concerns, a newborn baby, an unexpected job relocation, a pandemic, a divorce, or major financial issues.

No matter what it is, in that season, they may not be the same person to you they once were. In this case, you need to look at the relationship's history and patterns. If they were normally a great and supportive family member, friend, or co-worker, you shouldn't automatically write them off and deem the relationship unhealthy or toxic. You have to look at the circumstantial behavior and evidence. The person may need a little bit more love, support, and encouragement. They may need from YOU more of the healthy relationship components we talked about - trust, safety, honesty, respect, accountability, support, and cooperation - than they're able to provide.

We've talked about how harmony and reciprocity plays an important role in healthy interpersonal connections. Healthy relationships understand that there will be times where I need to show up a little bit more for you than you're able to show up for me. There are no hard feelings about that because we know that the tables always turn. Seasons are not forever. After a season ends, when your loved one could not show up for you like they normally would, that's when you can determine if this relationship needs to go on or not. However, if this person was mean, arrogant, lacked respect for your boundaries, and didn't have good communication skills, then maybe this isn't a difficult season for them, but perhaps it is a toxic and unhealthy relationship that you need to end immediately.

Resist the urge to write the relationship off as hard work, which as we previously discussed, will make you believe that it is too much work to show up for the person in a way they may not be able to show up for us. If you value the person and their relationship in your life, please do not think about giving them space and leaving them alone during this time and resuming things once their situation improves. I don't believe in ghosting people when they're experiencing hardship. If someone had a job loss or had a baby and they're going through postpartum, and you haven't heard from them in a long time or whatever the case may be, this isn't the time to ghost them. This is the time to try to be as supportive and amazing as possible.

Once the "season" ends, you can determine if this is something that you want to continue. If the answer is picking up on the healthy path where we left off, then cool! Let's proceed. If it is to end the relationship because it has been unhealthy, then it is time to act like an adult. Adults have to make hard decisions in life. You don't want to just ghost this person, block them, and no longer have them in your life. You want to attempt to end the relationship in a healthy manner. It may not be received well from them, but at least you can rest your head well at night on your pillow knowing, "I attempted to reach out to this person. I attempted to have a candid conversation with them, to be honest and truthful, and it wasn't received well." Then, it no longer becomes your problem. It is no longer your burden, and they must deal with their response or lack thereof. You did your part in the personal accountability area.

As a side note, I know there are people in some horrible, unsafe, toxic connections that need to be ended abruptly, and no final conversation needs to happen because of the potential for more physical or emotional damage. Do what your gut tells you to do. I know many of you may think blocking is harsh but let me tell you how strong my "block game" is. I will block someone from texting, calling, emailing, and contacting me via social media. You know I am serious when you get blocked from emailing me, too, lol. It is not to be mean or harsh, but it is to protect my peace. My peace is something I value at the highest level. I hope you realize there are things in your life that you CANNOT compromise. Stick to your values, do not compromise on them no matter what others may say.

Seasons are not time specific. A season could be a few days, a week, seven months, or three years. We're not talking about winter, spring, summer, or fall. We're talking about the different seasons in people's life where life throws them curveballs, and they're experiencing something that they didn't expect to experience. You have to trust yourself enough to know when the timing is right, based on the relationship and your history, to continue being there and supporting the person, so when it's over, they can say, "You were amazing during my time of need." Or you're going to end the relationship saying, "Hey, I didn't want to do this while you were down and out, but I don't think that this relationship is working for me. There's no reciprocity or harmony, and I would like to end it on good terms, if possible."

We are all human. There may be times when we need the same grace, compassion, love, respect, and empathy that others may need. At some point in our life, we will find ourselves being the ones who cannot give 100% in our relationships due to life throwing us a curveball. Treat others how you would like to be treated!

Reflection: Are the complex relationships in your life unhealthy or in a difficult season?

_____

_____

_____

_____

_____

_____

_____

_____

_____

_____

_____

_____

Hard Work or Harmony?

Bonus Chapter
HEAL YOURSELF TO BE HARMONIOUS WITH OTHERS

I could not write a book about healthy connections with family, friends, and co-workers without talking about the "F" word. No, I am not talking
about profanity. I am talking about FORGIVENESS.
I am sure you have heard the saying 'forgive and
forget.' Let me explain the power of both. Forgiveness is not for punks. It is a process that requires a
mature, heightened level of self-awareness because
you truly understand the benefits. When you have

been wronged by someone else, you have the right to feel sad, mad, frustrated, annoyed, and any other negative emotion. The key is to feel those emotions, deeply and intensely. I do not want you to suppress them because what you suppress, you cannot heal.

No one wants to be done wrong. Especially when you cannot understand why someone would treat you this way, it could be so many different reasons such as lies, betrayal, cheating, money being owed, disrespect, abuse, personality clashes, and the list goes on. These things can feel ten times worse when you have not done anything to deserve it. You were a good friend, a supportive co-worker, and a loving family member but still found yourself hurt by someone you cared about.

If you have not learned anything else from reading this book, I want you to remember that you cannot control other people. It is NOT our responsibility to police and monitor what other people do on a regular basis, no matter how right or wrong they are. The only thing that matters is YOU. How do YOU feel? What do YOU choose to say? What actions do

YOU choose to take? What thoughts are YOU having? It is all about you.

It is all about you because the power is in your hands. The desire to forgive and forget is up to you. What will you choose? No, it is not easy, and I am not forcing you to do anything you do not want to do or anything you are not ready to do. However, I want you to know that it is time to let it go. Be like the children's Disney movie Frozen and "Let it go! Let it gooooooooo!" It is not based on whether the other person deserves it or not because they may not. I can imagine that you are probably saying, "But Kiaundra! You do not know what they did to me." You are right! I have no clue.

What I do know is this: You are only punishing yourself. You are stopping your own healing from going forth. It is like YOU drinking poison but expecting the other person to die. It does not work that way. They are going on about their merry little lives while you are harboring pain, guilt, shame, anger, and resentment. It is consciously or unconsciously eating you up inside. I urge you to think deeply about it.

Unforgiveness has plagued many relationships because someone was too proud to admit they were wrong or felt like the other person should apologize first. I can't with that! That is so childish. Forgiveness is for those who want to take ownership of what they did and did not do.

Let's talk about what forgiveness is NOT. Just because you choose to forgive a loved one does not mean you have amnesia. It does not mean you forget everything that person has ever done to you, and now it has to be back like things were before. No! That is one of the biggest misconceptions about forgiveness. You do not have to subject yourself to the same foolery if there is no changed behavior on the other person's end. Sometimes, it is okay to love them from a distance. Meaning I have forgiven you, and I have no hard feelings. If I see you around, I can be cordial. I may have forgiven you, but I am not stupid—first time shame on you, second time shame on me. I will not allow you to get close enough to me to repeat the same offense twice. That is what happens when you forgive but do not forget.

If you are a person of faith, you already know how important forgiveness is to your livelihood and how it can be deadly. Unforgiveness can block you from receiving love, from going to the next level in your business; it can block your success, and it can make you literally sick. There is evidence to support that letting go of grudges, bitterness, resentment, and unforgiveness has significant health benefits. Forgiving another person is not for them; it is for you. You do not have to believe me; just try it. Once you try it, take notice of how much lighter and happier you are when you do not have unresolved issues lingering over your head. The goal is to be in a place where you forgive them even if you do not ever receive an apology.

Honestly, you may not even have to worry about forgiving other people because that is not your issue. The real issue may be forgiving *yourself*. Yes, I said it. You may be walking around with unresolved issues with yourself and thinking that it is not affecting you. But guess what? It is! It is not only affecting you but affecting those closest to you. It is possible to forgive yourself for the mistakes you made. You can forgive yourself for getting that abortion, ending the marriage that did not work, not being present for your children's extracurricular activities, putting your business before your family, not going to the doctor sooner, or neglecting your mental health because you were trying to be everything to everyone. Finding harmony in your relationships and with the different components of yourself can be a life-long journey. However, it is a necessary one.

There is freedom and forgiveness for you too. All you have to do is want it. The "how-to" part comes later. You do not have to figure it all out now. All you have to do is declare that you, too, want to be whole.

Final Thought

There is a huge chance that this book only scratched the surface of what you need for more in-depth healing in your connections with others. Your learning and growing does not stop here. You can take this information into the real world and apply it. How many times have we read books and watched videos that were transformational? But, we failed to apply any of the principles, concepts, tips, or golden nuggets to our lives and wonder why things are still the same.

My job is to hold you accountable. You are in a completely different place than others who may also be reading this book. Take note of where you are and where you desire to be, then commit to applying the techniques shared in the book to help you live the life you desire.

For some, this is the end of the road. This book gave you exactly what you needed to enhance your interpersonal relationships. For others, this is only the beginning, and you will need to seek other books, classes, and maybe even some professional help to better your overall life. No matter where you find yourself, remember everyone has to start somewhere. Slow progress is still progress.

I am committed to providing resources that will help you along the journey. Stay tuned for more life-changing books to come.

Feel free to visit me at www.KiaundraJackson. com for resources and upcoming events and follow me on social media to stay connected:

@KiaundraJackson

Notes

Chapter 1: CONNECTED BY BLOOD, CHOICE, OR MARRIAGE

1. Definition of Harmony. Dictionary.com. https://www.dictionary.com/browse/harmony

Chapter 2: THE RELEVANCE OF RELATIONSHIPS

2. "The 8 Different Types of Love and the Perfect Combo for You," FTD.com. https://www.ftd.com/blog/give/types-of-love

3. "US Experiment on Infants Withholding Affection" Discussion by St. Paul's Collegiate School Hamilton. https://stpauls.vxcommunity.com/Issue/us-experiment-oninfants-withholding-affection/13213

Bonus Chapter: PERSONALITY TYPES AFFECT PERSONAL RELATIONSHIPS

4. 16 Personality Type Descriptions and Quiz, www.16personalities.com

5. "Big Five Personality Test Traits," Dr. Edwin van Thiel. 123test.com https://www.123test.com/big-five-personality-theory/

Chapter 5: HOPING FOR HARMONY

6. "The 5 Love Languages and What They

Mean," CratedwithLove.com. https://crated-withlove.com/blog/five-love-languages-and-what-they-mean/

Bonus Chapter: RELATIONSHIP RULES FOR INTROVERTS AND EXTROVERTS

7. "Mind: Introverted vs. Extroverted," 16Personalities.com. https://www.16personalities.com/articles/mind-introverted-vs-extraverted

8. "What is an Ambivert? Take the Quiz to See if You Are an Introvert, Extrovert or Ambivert," Vanessa Van Edward. ScienceofPeople.com. https://www.scienceofpeople.com/ambivert/

About the Author

Kiaundra Jackson is known as America's #1 Relationship Therapist. She has been seen on OWN's hit TV Show, Love Goals and as a recurring expert on The Doctors. Kiaundra has been recently featured in Oprah's Magazine, Essence, The New York Times, FOX, The CW, BET, Women's Health Magazine and The HuffPost as one of the '10 Black Female Therapists You Should Know.' She is an award-winning speaker, best-selling author, TV Personality and a trusted Licensed Marriage and Family Therapist that gets results. She is a noted expert on healthy relationships and mental health. Kiaundra is the visionary of KW Couples Therapy and the Co-Founder of Black Speakers Rock.

To book Kiaundra for your next speaking engagement, conference, workshop, or training, please send you request to:

Kiaundra@KWCouplesTherapy.com

Other Books by Kiaundra:

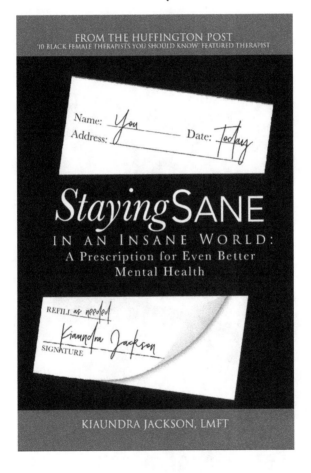

www.StayingSaneWorld.com

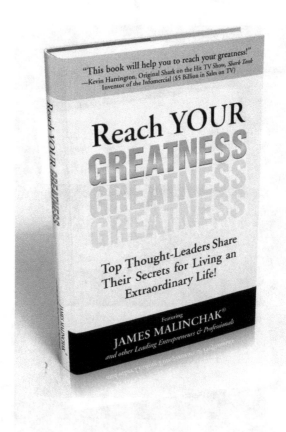

www.KiaundraJackson.com

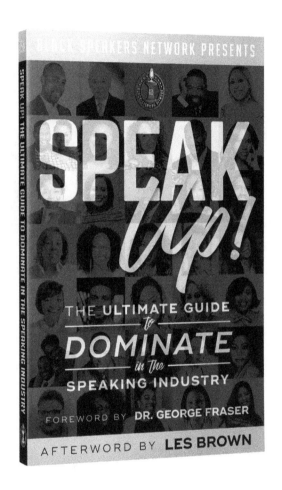

www.KiaundraJackson.com

CPSIA information can be obtained
at www.ICGtesting.com
Printed in the USA
BVHW041414231120
593969BV00015B/1429